MY BOOK

Published by UnilX Education

books@unilxeducation.com
USA +1 619 798 6274
MEX +52 6631030487

MyEnglishGameZone®, 2021 ©UnilX LLC, 2021

First Published 2021

Author: Patricia Armida Ávila Delfín
Editor: Sandra Rojas
Main Characters: My English Game Zone®
Cover and Complimentary Graphics: UnilX, Innovalingua Design Team and Freepik.com
Illustration, Design and Animation Leader: Rafael Orellana
Editorial Design: UNIGRÁPHICA, UnilX editorial team, Rafael Orellana

PROGRAM SYNOPSIS

The fundamental objective of **My English Zone The Book** is learning to communicate through interaction in the target language. The Theory of Language learning tells us that "language is a tool for communication and that students learn a language by using it to communicate."

You will find that **My English Zone The Book** is a series based on guided everyday communicative interaction. E.g. when students are faced with real life dialogs to find out the schedule of the week's exams or to describe a classmate by his/her physical appearance, among many other authentic situations. Guided dialogs provide opportunities for language learners to interact with each other or with native speakers while feeling comfortable doing so.

This series also acknowledges the role of grammar as that of great importance for our learners to reach higher levels of proficiency and introduces the basic structures from the start of the program.

My English Zone The Book also makes extensive use of authentic texts like: songs, jokes, rhymes, tongue twisters and popular children's stories. They will enrich the knowledge of culture through language.

As you can see, **My English Zone The Book** has a solid base on the most important methodologies necessary to enhance the learning of the second language in a dynamic and fun way.

Patricia Avila Delfín

SERIES FEATURES

- Each book with 15 units.
- Each unit has five lessons:

Book number	CEFR
1	Pre-A1
2	Pre-A1
3	A1.1
4	A1.2
5	A2.1
6	A2.1
7	A2.2
8	A2.2
9	B1.1
10	B1.2
11	B1.3
12	B1+

Lesson 1: Vocabulary
In this first lesson the vocabulary that will be used during the rest of the unit will be presented through clear images that represent each word.

Lesson 2: Dialogs
The dialogs will recap the vocabulary items from lesson one and use them in everyday real situations.

Lesson 3: Reading
The reading texts will go from original stories that take the ideas of the dialogs and complete them in a text to popular stories from children's literature.

Lesson 4: Writing
Prompted writing is used in the lower levels. It encourages students to use their imagination to come up with new and creative ideas for the text. In the higher levels, students will be asked to arrange the paragraphs or the missing sentences to complete the stories they read before.

Lesson 5: Language in Use
The last part of each unit, recaps the grammar structures seen, through the presentation of language in use of the four lessons before it. There are activities that will evaluate the knowledge acquired.

Vocabulary Learning

Vocabulary learning is central to language acquisition.

Specialists emphasize the need for a systematic and principled approach of vocabulary by the teacher and the learner. Teaching techniques and activities state that new words should not be learned by simple rote memorization.

It is important that new vocabulary items be presented in contexts rich enough to provide clues to meaning and that students be given multiple exposure to items they should learn.

Communicative Language Learning

Learning to communicate through interaction in the target language is the principal characteristic of the Communicative Language Teaching approach.

The The*ory of Language Learning states that:*
• *Langu*age is a tool for communication
• Students learn a language by using it to communicate

Integrated Skills Approach

The four basic skills in language teaching are: listening, speaking, reading , writing .

When we acquire a second language in a natural way the skills appear in that same order.

But why should we integrate the four skills when teaching the second language? If we are focused on teaching a realistic communication competence, the four skills must be developed in an integrated way .

 Integrating the skills allows us to use more variety in the lessons because the range of activities will be ampler.

Spiral Learning

Learning should work like a game in a spiral, that gets a child interested while repeating and gradually increasing difficulty. It also gives students challenging activities and at the same time adds new skills.

The steps to achieve Spiral Learning are:
•   Introduce new language. Move forward.
•   Recap the important language learned so far.
•   Add more language.
•   Recap selected language: recent and earlier.
•   Repeat the process.

Topic Based Approach

Topic based approach is student-centered. It helps with students' attention span.
It will hold students' interest from the start to the end of the lesson.

CONTENTS MAP

MY PLATFORM ACCESS

URL: _____

User name: _____

Password: _____

Ask your teacher or parents if you have a platform access.

Learn the countries

 USA    England   France   Japan    Mexico

1 one	2 two	3 three	4 four	5 five
6 six	7 seven	8 eight	9 nine	10 ten
11 eleven	12 twelve	13 thirteen	14 fourteen	15 fifteen
16 sixteen	17 seventeen	18 eighteen	19 nineteen	20 twenty

A a	B b	C c	D d	E e
F f	G g	H h	I i	J j
K k	L l	M m	N n	O o
P p	Q q	R r	S s	T t
U u	V v	W w	X x	Y y
Z z				

Practice the dialogs

Good morning!
What's your name?
-My name is Michelle.
How do you spell it?
-M-I-C-H-E-L-L-E
How old are you?
-I'm 7 years old.
Where are you from?
-I'm from France.

Good morning!
What's your name?
-My name is Akiko.
How do you spell it?
A-K-I-K-O
How old are you?
-I'm 7 years old.
Where are you from?
-I'm from Japan.

Good morning!
What's your name?
-My name is Harry.
How do you spell it?
-H-A-R-R-Y
How old are you?
-I'm 8 years old.
Where are you from?
-I'm from England.

Good morning!
What's your name?
-My name is Tom.
How do you spell it?
-T-O-M
How old are you?
-I'm 8 years old.
Where are you from?
-I'm from the USA.

Good morning!
What's your name?
-My name is Rosa.
How do you spell it?
-R-O-S-A
How old are you?
-I'm 8 years old.
Where are you from?
-I'm from Mexico.

Now you!

Good morning!
What's your name?
-My name is _____.
How do you spell it?
-___ ___ ___ ___ ___ ___ ___ ___
How old are you?
-I'm _____ years old.
Where are you from?
-I'm from _____.

New friends

There are new friends at school.
They are Michelle, Akiko, Harry and Tom.
Michelle is 7 years old; she isn't from
England, she's from France.
Akiko is 7 years old; she isn't from the USA,
she's from Japan.
Harry is 8 years old; he isn't from France,
he's from England.
Tom is 8 years old; he isn't from Japan,
he's from the USA.
Welcome to our school new friends!

Where are they from?

1. Where is Tom from?

   ❑ France   ❑ USA   ❑ Japan

2. Where is Akiko from?

   ❑ France   ❑ USA   ❑ Japan

3. Where is Harry from?

   ❑ England   ❑ France   ❑ USA

4. Where is Michelle from?

   ❑ England   ❑ Japan   ❑ France

Read the sentences and circle true or false

1. Tom is seven years old.

   True   False

2. Akiko is from France.

   True   False

3. Harry is from England.

   True   False

4. Michelle is from Japan.

   True   False

5. Tom is from England.

   True   False

Complete the reading with the words from the box below in any order and times you think necessary.

New friends

There are new friends at school.
They are Michelle, Akiko, Harry and Tom.
Michelle is _____ years old; she isn't from _____,
she's from _____.
Akiko is _____ years old; she isn't from _____,
she's from _____.
Harry is _____ years old; he isn't from _____,
he's from _____.
Tom is _____ years old; he isn't from _____,
he's from _____.
Welcome to our school new friends!

---

5 • 6 • 7 • 8 • 9 • 10
France • the USA • Japan • England

Present Simple Tense verb BE
We use the verb **BE** in the Present Simple to talk about
names, professions, nationalities, age and feelings.

Affirmative form:
I **am**
He/she/it **is**
We/you/they **are**

Interrogative form:
Am I?
Is he/she/it?
Are you/they/we?

Negative form:
I **am+not**
He/she/it **is+not**
We/you/they **are+not**

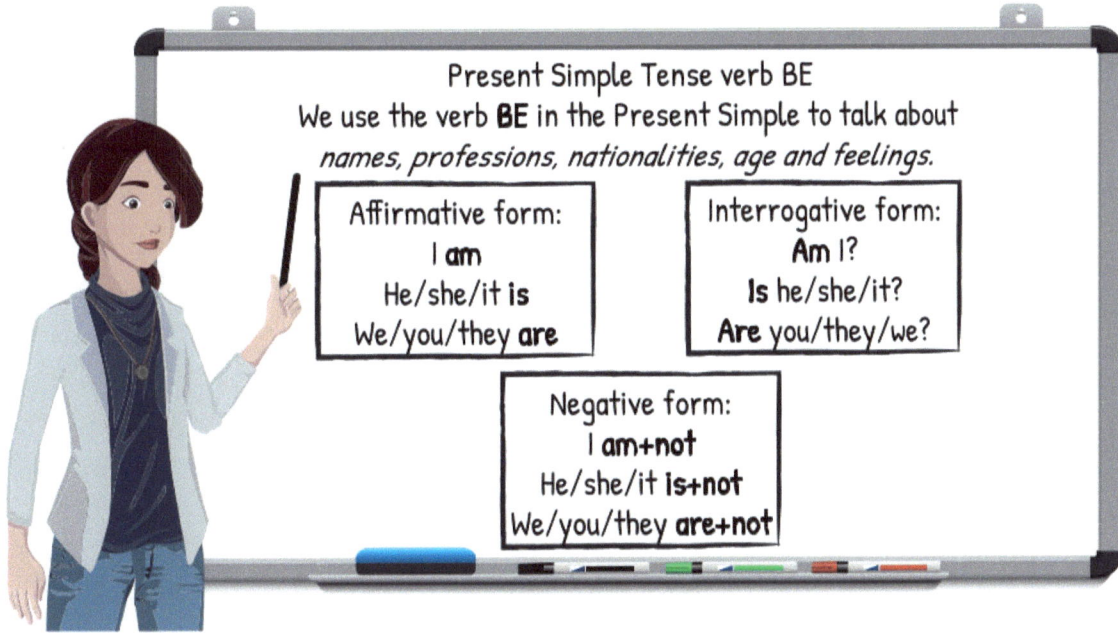

Unscramble the sentences

1. ____ ____ ____ ____ .
   isn't / Japan / from / he

2. ____ ____ ____ ____ ____
   ? / they / England / from / are

3. ____ ____ ____ ____ ____
   name / is / ? / what / your

4. ____ ____ ____ ____ .
   we / France / aren't / from

5. ____ ____ ____ ____ .
   I / am / Mexico / from

Complete the sentences.

1. Akiko _____ from Japan.

2. Harry _____ from the USA.

3. Where _____ they from?

4. _____ is your name?

5. Michelle and Antoine _____
   from England.

What • are • aren't • is • isn't

How well did you do in this unit?

_____

Write the CAN DO statement and assess yourself:

I can...

_____
_____
_____

Review the rooms in the house and family members

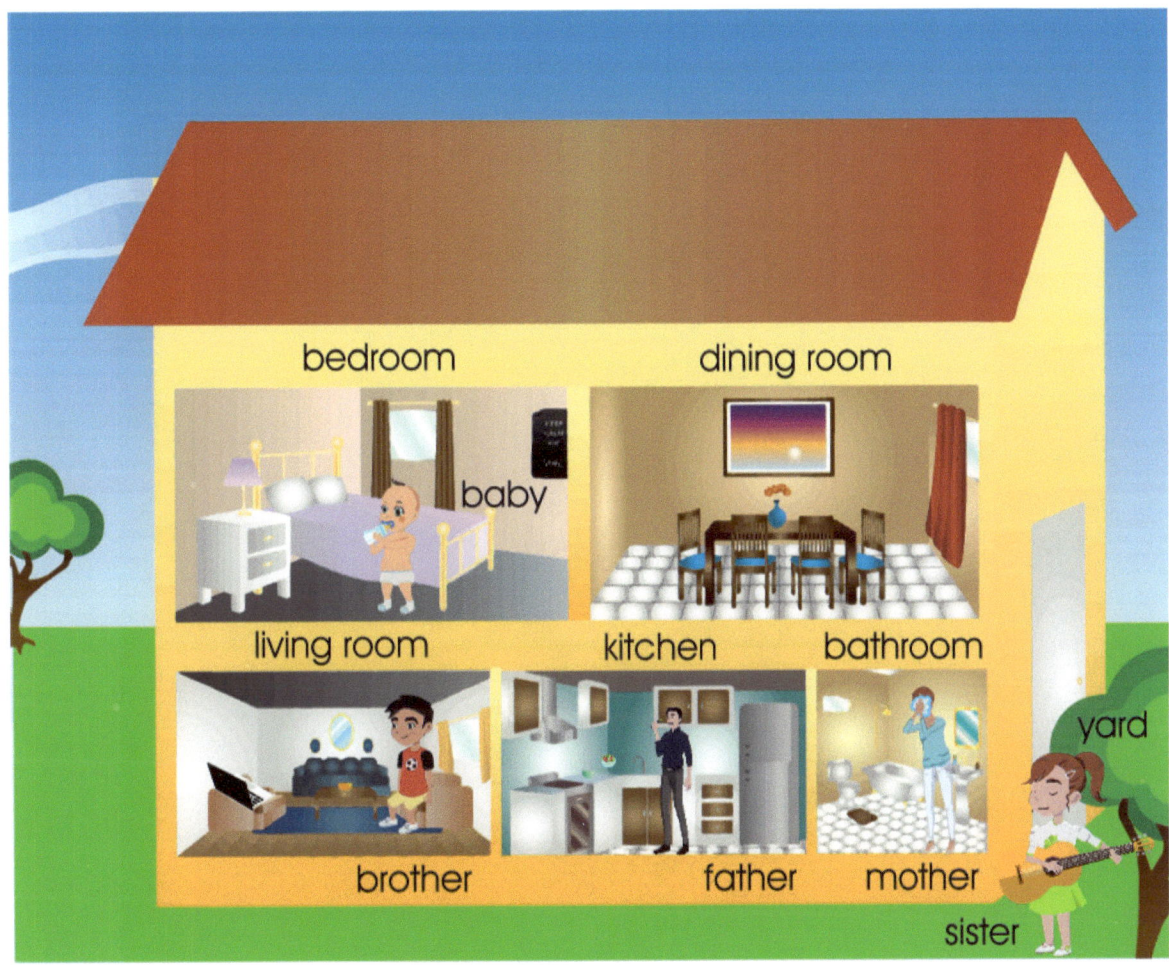

Practice the dialogs

Where is mother?
-She is in the bathroom.
Is she washing her hands?
-No, she isn't. She's washing her face.

Where is father?
He's in the kitchen.
Is he eating a sandwich?
No, he isn't. He's eating salad.

Where is baby?
He's in the bedroom.
Is he sleeping?
No, he isn't. He's drinking milk.

Where is sister?
She's in the yard.
Is she playing soccer?
No, she isn't. She's playing the guitar.

Now you!

Where is _____?
He's in the _____.
Is he _____?
No, he isn't. He's _____.

At home

All my family is at home today.
Father is in the kitchen, he's eating salad.
Mother is in the bathroom, she's washing her face.
Brother is in the living room, he's watching videos.
Sister is in the yard, she's playing the guitar.
Baby is in the bedroom, he's drinking milk.
And what am I doing? I am writing this story.
I love my family!

Where are they?

1. Where is mother?
   ❑ kitchen ❑ yard ❑ bathroom
2. Where is father?
   ❑ kitchen ❑ yard ❑ bathroom
3. Where is sister?
   ❑ kitchen ❑ yard ❑ bathroom
4. Where is baby?
   ❑ bedroom ❑ yard
   ❑ living room
5. Where is brother?
   ❑ bedroom ❑ yard
   ❑ living room

Answer the questions

1. What is mother doing?
   _____.
2. What is father doing?
   _____.
3. What is baby doing?
   _____.
4. What is sister doing?
   _____.
5. What is brother doing?
   _____.

Complete the text with the words from the box below. In any order you think necessary.

At home

All my family is at home today.
Father is in the _____, he's _____.
Mother is in the _____, she's _____.
Brother is in the _____, he's _____.
Sister is in the _____, she's _____.
Baby is in the _____, he's _____.
And what am I doing? I am _____.
I love my family!

---

kitchen • living room • yard • bedroom • bathroom
washing face • eating salad • drinking milk
watching videos • playing guitar • writing the story

Present Progressive Tense.
The present progressive tense expresses a current action, an action in progress.

We use the verb **BE** as a helping verb.
In sentences with HE, SHE, IT we use the verb **IS**.

To make a question we put **IS** before the pronoun.
Is he coloring?

To make negative sentences we use **IS + NOT**
He **is not** (isn't) playing.

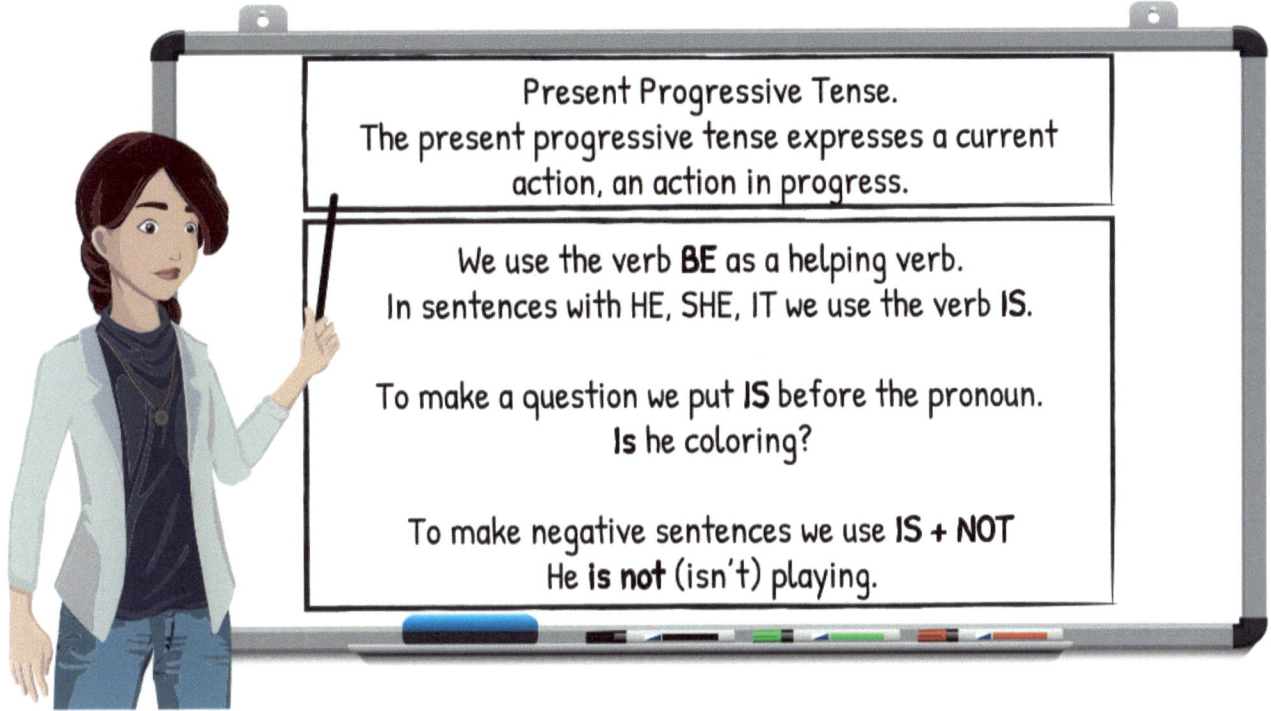

Change the sentences into questions

1. Mother is in the bathroom.
   _____?

2. Father is in the kitchen.
   _____?

3. Brother is in the living room.
   _____?

4. Sister is in the yard.
   _____?

5. Baby is the bedroom.
   _____?

Change the sentences into negative

1. Mother is in the bathroom.
   _____.

2. Father is in the kitchen.
   _____.

3. Brother is in the living room.
   _____.

4. Sister is in the yard.
   _____.

5. Baby is the bedroom.
   _____.

How well did you do in this unit?

Write the CAN DO statement and assess yourself:

I can...

Review the animals and where they live

FARM

 donkey

 horse

cow

ZOO

 tiger

 lion

bear

HOME

 cat

dog

hamster

Practice the dialogs

What is that?
-It's a lion.
Does a lion live in the farm?
-No, it doesn't. It lives in the zoo.

What are those?
-Those are donkeys.
Do donkeys live in the zoo?
-No, they don't. They live in the farm.

What is that?
-It's a cow.
Does a cow live in the zoo?
-No, it doesn't. It lives in the farm.

What are those?
-Those are cats.
Do cats live in the zoo?
-No, they don't. They live in a home.

What is that?
-It's a hamster.
Does a hamster live in the farm?
-No, it doesn't. It lives in a home.

Now you!

What are those?
-Those are _____.
Do _____ live in the _____?
-No, they don't. They live in a _____.

What is that?
-It's a _____.
Does a _____ live in the _____?
-No, it doesn't. It lives in a _____.

Animals, animals, animals!

Different animals live in different places.
Lions, tigers and bears don't live in homes and they
don't live in farms. Where do they live?
They live in the zoo.
Horses, donkeys and cows don't live in homes, and
they don't live in the zoo. Where do they live?
They live in the farm.
Cats, dogs and hamsters don't live in the zoo and
they don't live in the farm. Where do they live?
They live in homes.
What animals live in your home?

Answer the questions

1. The lion lives in the:
   ❑ zoo ❑ farm ❑ home
2. The hamster lives in the:
   ❑ zoo ❑ farm ❑ home
3. Cats live in the:
   ❑ zoo ❑ farm ❑ home
4. Bears live in the:
   ❑ zoo ❑ farm ❑ home
5. The donkey lives in the:
   ❑ zoo ❑ farm ❑ home

Read the sentences
Circle true (✔) or false (✗)

1. Bears live in the home. ✔ ✗
2. Cats live in the zoo. ✔ ✗
3. Lions live in the farm. ✔ ✗
4. The hamster lives in the home. ✔ ✗
5. The cow lives in the farm. ✔ ✗
6. The horse lives in the farm. ✔ ✗

Complete the reading with the words from the box below

Animals, animals, animals!

Different animals live in different places.
Lions don't live in the _____
and they don't live in the _____ .
Where do they live? They live in the _____ .
Dogs don't live in the _____ ,
and they don't live in the _____ .
Where do they live? They live in the _____ .
A cow doesn't live in the _____
and it doesn't live in the _____ .
Where does it live? It lives in the _____ .

What is your favorite animal, where does it live?

---

farm (x3) • zoo (x3) • home (x3)

Present Simple Tense
We can express **habits**, **customs** and **routines** with the Present Simple Tense.

In the third person singular we add an "S" at the end of the verb.
A police officer helps people.

We use the helping verb **DO/ DOES** to make interrogative sentences.
We use the helping verb **DO/DOES + NOT** to make negative sentences.

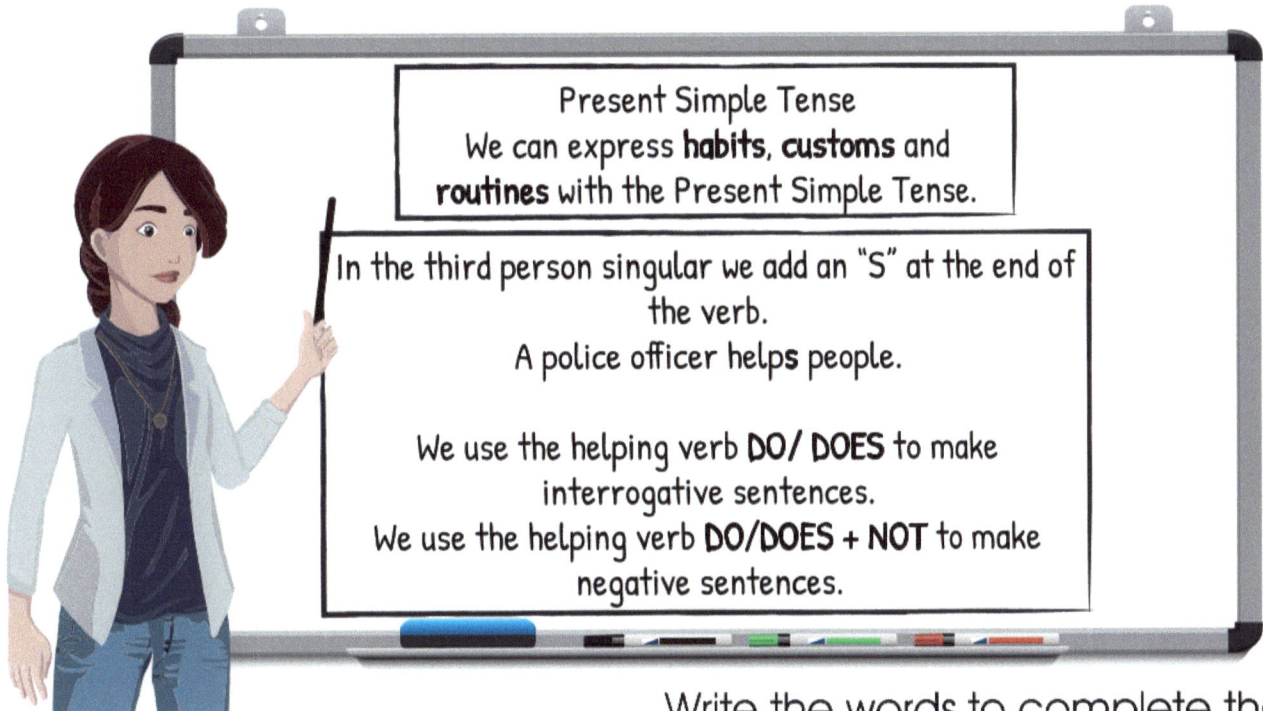

Choose the correct word

1. Lions _____ in the zoo.
   • live   • lives

2. _____ tigers live in the zoo?
   • Do   • Does

3. Where _____ a bear live?
   • do   • does

4. A hamster _____ live in the farm.
   • don't   • doesn't

5. Cats _____ live in the zoo.
   • don't   • doesn't

6. Where _____ cows live?
   • do   • doesn't

Write the words to complete the sentences

1. A lion _____ live in the farm.

2. Cats _____ live in the zoo.

3. _____ a horse live in the farm?

4. _____ donkeys live in the farm?

5. A dog _____ in the home.

6. Bears _____ in the zoo.

do • does • live
lives • doesn't • don't

23

How well did you do in this unit?

_____

Write the CAN DO statement and assess yourself:

I can...

_____

_____

_____

_____

_____

_____

Learn the year celebrations!

Calendar

January
S	M	T	W	T	F	S
		1	2	3	4	5
6	7	8	9	10	11	12
13	14	15	16	17	18	19
20	21	22	23	24	25	26
27	28	29	30	31		

New Year's Day

February
S	M	T	W	T	F	S
					1	2
3	4	5	6	7	8	9
10	11	12	13	14	15	16
17	18	19	20	21	22	23
24	25	26	27	28		

Valentine's Day

March
S	M	T	W	T	F	S
					1	2
3	4	5	6	7	8	9
10	11	12	13	14	15	16
17	18	19	20	21	22	23
24	25	26	27	28	29	30
31						

April
S	M	T	W	T	F	S
	1	2	3	4	5	6
7	8	9	10	11	12	13
14	15	16	17	18	19	20
21	22	23	24	25	26	27
28	29	30				

May
S	M	T	W	T	F	S
			1	2	3	4
5	6	7	8	9	10	11
12	13	14	15	16	17	18
19	20	21	22	23	24	25
26	27	28	29	30	31	

Mother's Day

June
S	M	T	W	T	F	S
						1
2	3	4	5	6	7	8
9	10	11	12	13	14	15
16	17	18	19	20	21	22
23	24	25	26	27	28	29

July
S	M	T	W	T	F	S
	1	2	3	4	5	6
7	8	9	10	11	12	13
14	15	16	17	18	19	20
21	22	23	24	25	26	27
28	29	30	31			

August
S	M	T	W	T	F	S
				1	2	3
4	5	6	7	8	9	10
11	12	13	14	15	16	17
18	19	20	21	22	23	24
25	26	27	28	29	30	31

September
S	M	T	W	T	F	S
1	2	3	4	5	6	7
8	9	10	11	12	13	14
15	16	17	18	19	20	21
22	23	24	25	26	27	28
29	30					

October
S	M	T	W	T	F	S
		1	2	3	4	5
6	7	8	9	10	11	12
13	14	15	16	17	18	19
20	21	22	23	24	25	26
27	28	29	30	31		

Halloween

November
S	M	T	W	T	F	S
					1	2
3	4	5	6	7	8	9
10	11	12	13	14	15	16
17	18	19	20	21	22	23
24	25	26	27	28	29	30

Thanksgiving

December
S	M	T	W	T	F	S
1	2	3	4	5	6	7
8	9	10	11	12	13	14
15	16	17	18	19	20	21
22	23	24	25	26	27	28
29	30	31				

Christmas

Practice the dialogs

Mother's Day is going to be next week, are you ready?
-Sure!

-Halloween is going to be next Tuesday, are you ready?
-Almost!

Thanksgiving is going to be next month, are you ready?
-No, not yet!

The Christmas Ball is going to be next weekend, are you ready?
-Of course!

Valentine's Day is going to be next Friday, are you ready?
-Totally!

_____ is going to be next _____, are you ready?
-_____!

Now you!

Let's celebrate!

Next year I am going to have fun at many celebrations.
We are going to start on January 1st,
we are going to celebrate New Year's Day.
On February 14th, we are going to celebrate
Valentine's Day at school.
In May, I am going to dance in a Mother's Day festival.
Halloween is going to be fun, I am going to dress up
as a Super-Hero!
In November my family and I are going to visit my grandma
and we are going to eat a big Thanksgiving dinner.
And the last celebration is on December 25th,
Christmas Day, I love Christmas!
What celebration is your favorite?

What holiday is it?

1. December 25th is:
   - ☐ Christmas Day
   - ☐ Valentine's Day
   - ☐ Halloween
2. May 10th is:
   - ☐ Christmas Day
   - ☐ Mother's Day
   - ☐ Halloween
3. 3rd Thursday in November is:
   - ☐ Mother's Day
   - ☐ Valentine's Day
   - ☐ Thanksgiving
4. February 14th is:
   - ☐ Valentine's Day
   - ☐ Thanksgiving
   - ☐ Mother's Day

Read the sentences.
Circle true (✔) or false (✘)

1. Christmas is December 25th.

   ✔   ✘

2. New Year's Day is in November.

   ✔   ✘

3. Mother's Day is in May.

   ✔   ✘

4. Valentine's Day is in January.

   ✔   ✘

5. Halloween is October, 31st.

   ✔   ✘

Complete the reading with the words from the box below. Choose the correct holiday.

Let's celebrate!

Next year I am going to have fun at many celebrations.
We are going to start on January 1st,
we are going to celebrate _____.
On February 14th,
we are going to celebrate _____ at school.
In May, I am going to dance in a _____ festival.
_____ is going to be fun,
I am going to dress up as a Super-Hero!
In November my family and I are going to visit
my grandma and we are going to eat a big
_____ dinner.
And the last celebration is on December 25th,
_____. I love it!

What celebration is your favorite?

Christmas • Halloween • Mother´s Day • New Year´s Day
Valentine´s Day • Thanksgiving Day

Future Tense Affirmative

We use **BE** + going to + verb to express a planned action in the future.

Affirmative sentences:
I **am** going to dress-up as a super hero!
We **are** going to visit grandma.
She **is** going to dance in the festival.

Time to Rhyme!

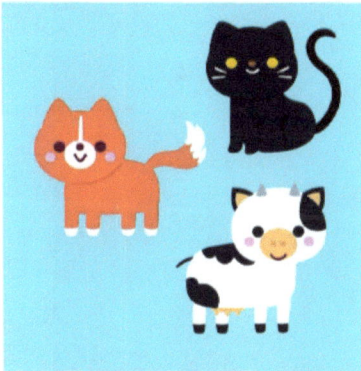

Hey diddle diddle,
The cat and the fiddle,
The cow jumped over
the moon,
The little dog laughed
To see such fun,
And the dish ran away
with the spoon!

Unscramble the sentences

1. _____ _____ _____ _____
going to / next weekend / is
Christmas / be

2. _____ _____ _____ _____
Next Friday / going to / Valentine's
Day / be

3. _____ _____ _____ _____
_____ .
is / Thanksgiving / going to / next
month /be

4. _____ _____ _____ _____
next week / be / going to / is
Mother's Day

How well did you do in this unit?

Write the CAN DO statement and assess yourself:

I can...

Learn the names of the food!

DELICIOUS RESTAURANT MENU

Breakfast:
- eggs .... $ 4.00
- bread ...... $ 2.00
- cereal ..... $ 1.50

Lunch:
- sandwich .. $ 3.50
- salad .... $ 4.50

Dinner:
- chicken .... $ 4.75
- meat .... $ 6.00
- fish .... $ 5.50

Drinks:
- water .... $ 1.50
- juice .... $ 2.00

Find the words

X	D	P	E	P	W	C	S	D	Y
F	L	A	K	G	H	Q	A	E	J
I	C	Q	E	I	G	L	N	C	P
S	W	S	C	R	A	S	D	I	R
H	E	K	N	S	B	D	W	U	S
F	E	W	A	T	E	R	I	J	W
N	L	A	E	R	E	C	C	O	M
D	J	P	F	W	H	W	H	E	Q
F	N	I	V	Z	L	J	A	Y	N
I	F	A	M	Z	X	T	F	K	H

BREAD
CEREAL
CHICKEN
EGGS
FISH
JUICE
MEAT
SALAD
SANDWICH
WATER

Practice the dialogs

Are you going to eat our delicious sandwich and water?
-Yes, I am. Thank you.

Are Lucy and Tony going to eat the delicious eggs and bread?
-Yes, they are. Thank you.

Are you and Andy going to choose our delicious chicken and salad?
-Yes, we are. Thank you.

Is Sandy going to have fish and water?
-Yes, she is. Thank you.

Is Harry going to taste our delicious meat and juice?
-Yes, he is. Thank you.

Now you!

Is/Are _____ going to _____
_____?
-Yes, ___ ___ . Thank you.

The delicious restaurant

My friends and I are going to celebrate my birthday at the "Delicious Restaurant". It is our favorite place to eat! Lucy and Tony are going to eat eggs and bread. Andy is going to choose chicken and salad. Sandy is going to have fish and water. Harry is going to taste meat and juice. Akiko and Tom are going to have cereal and juice. And I am going to have my favorite, a sandwich and tasty water! I love the Delicious Restaurant it is my favorite place to eat.

What are they gong to eat?

1. Andy is going to choose:
   - ❑ chicken and salad
   - ❑ fish and water
   - ❑ cereal and juice
2. Lucy and Tony are going to eat:
   - ❑ fish and salad.
   - ❑ eggs and bread
   - ❑ cereal and juice
3. Harry is going to taste:
   - ❑ cereal and juice
   - ❑ fish and juice
   - ❑ meat and juice
4. Akiko and Tom are going to have:
   - ❑ cereal and juice
   - ❑ chicken and salad
   - ❑ eggs and bread

Match the sentences with the food

1. Andy is going to choose: (____)
2. Lucy and Tony are going to eat: (____)
3. Harry is going to eat: (____)
4. Akiko and Tom are going to have: (____)
5. I am going to have: (____)

a) Meat and juice
b) Sandwich and water
c) Eggs and bread
d) Chicken and salad
e) Cereal and juice

Complete the reading with the words from the box below

The delicious restaurant

My friends and I are going to celebrate my birthday
at the "Delicious Restaurant".
It is our favorite place to eat!
Lucy and Tony are going to eat _____.
Andy is going to choose _____.
Sandy is going to have _____. Harry is going to taste _____.
Akiko and Tom are going to have _____.
And I am going to have my favorite, a _____!
I love the Delicious Restaurant it is my favorite place to eat.

Chicken and salad • Eggs and bread • Meat and juice
Cereal and juice • Sandwich and water • Fish and water

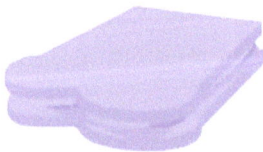

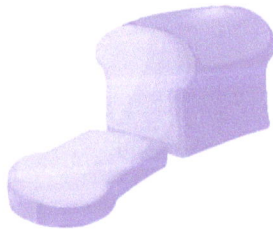

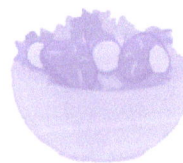

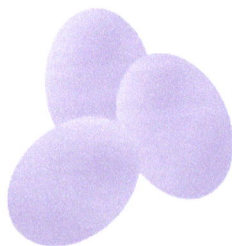

Future Tense Interrogative

We use **BE** + going to + verb to express a planned action in the future.

Interrogative sentences:
BE+ subject+ going to+ verb?
Are you going to eat bread and juice?
Are they going to have fish and juice?
Is she going to choose cereal and juice?

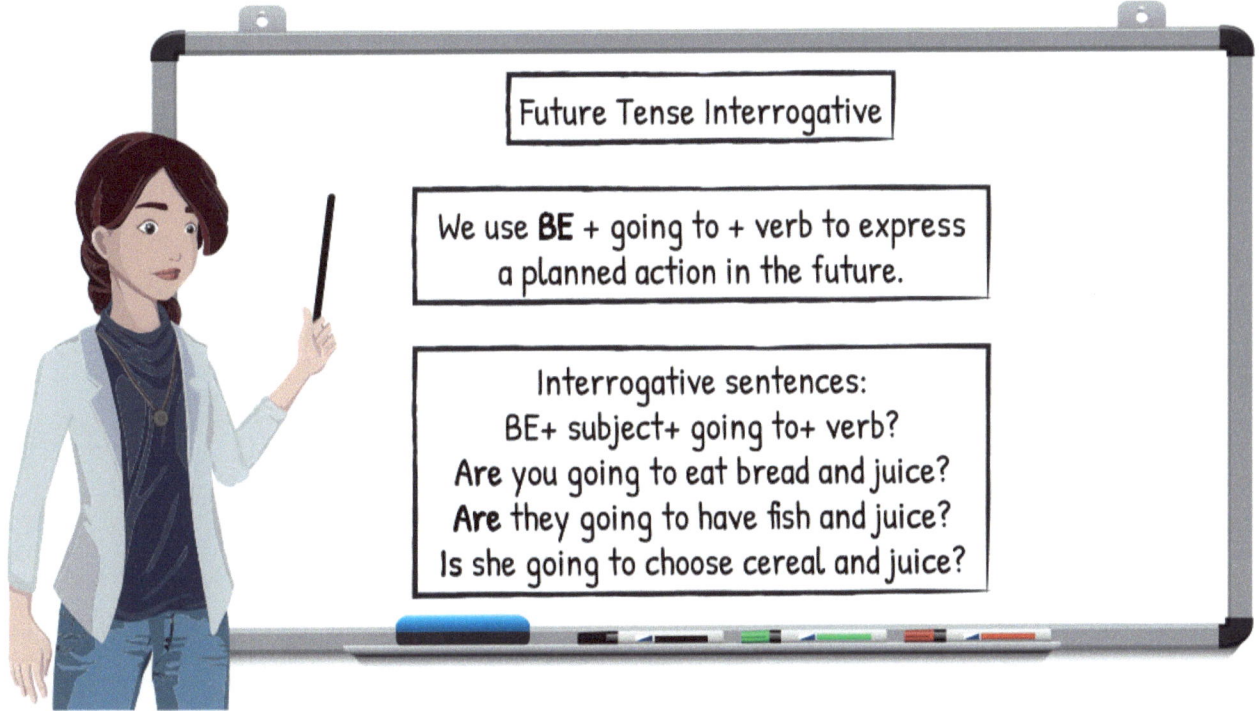

Write a short affirmative answer

1. Are they going to eat fish?

_____ _____ _____

2. Are you and Andy going to choose eggs?

_____ _____ _____

3. Are you going to eat chicken?

_____ _____ _____

4. Is Sandy going to have a sandwich?

_____ _____ _____

5. Is Tony going to drink water?

_____ _____ _____

Unscramble the sentences

1. ___ ___ ___ ___ ___ ___?
a sandwich/eat/going/to/you/are

2. ___ ___ ___ ___ ___?
they/eat/going to/eggs/are

3. ___ ___ ___ ___ ___?
chicken/going to/you/are choose

4. ___ ___ ___ ___ ___?
fish/going to/she /is/have

5. ___ ___ ___ ___ ___?
they/are/going to/cereal have

How well did you do in this unit?

_____

Write the CAN DO statement and assess yourself:

I can...

_____

_____

_____

_____

_____

_____

_____

_____

_____

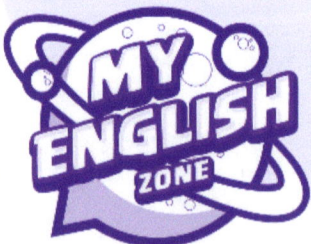

Learn the names of the school supplies!

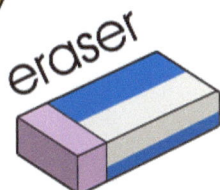

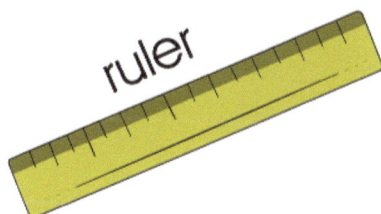

book

notebook

pencil

sharpener

eraser

crayons

marker

color pencils

ruler

pen

Practice the dialogs

Is Sandy going to write with a pen tomorrow?
-Yes, she is.
-She isn't going to write with a pencil.

Is Lucy going to color with color pencils tomorrow?
-Yes, she is.
-She isn't going to color with crayons.

Is Tony going to use a new sharpener tomorrow?
-Yes, he is.
-He isn't going to use a new eraser.

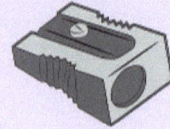

Are you going to work in the book tomorrow?
-Yes, I am.
-I'm not going to work in the notebook.

Now you!

Are you going to _____
 tomorrow?
-Yes, I am.
-I'm not going to _____.

Busy day at school

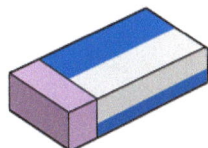

Tomorrow is going to be a busy day at school.
Sandy isn't going to write with a pencil
but she is going to write with a pen.
Lucy isn't going to color with crayons
but she's going to color with color pencils.
Tony isn't going to use a new eraser
but he's going to use a new sharpener.
Andy isn't going to borrow a marker
but he's going to borrow a ruler.
And, I am not going to work in the notebook
but I am going to work in the book.
Yes, tomorrow is going to be a very busy day at school!

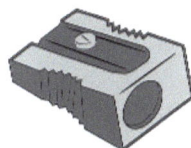

What are they going to do tomorrow?

1. Is Sandy going to write with a pencil?
❏ Yes, she is. ❏ No, she isn't.
2. Is Lucy going to color with color pencils?
❏ Yes, she is. ❏ No, she isn't.
3. Is Tony going to use a new eraser?
❏ Yes, she is. ❏ No, she isn't.
4. Is Andy going to borrow a marker?
❏ Yes, she is. ❏ No, she isn't.
5. Are you going to work in the book?
❏ Yes, I am. ❏ No, I'm not.

Answer true or false

1. Sandy is going to write with a pencil.
❏ True ❏ False
2. Lucy is going to color with color pencils.
❏ True ❏ False
3. Tony is going to use a new sharpener.
❏ True ❏ False
4. Andy is going to borrow a ruler.
❏ True ❏ False
5. I am going to work in the book.
❏ True ❏ False

Choose a word from the box below and fill in a blank. Then read aloud.

Busy day at school

Tomorrow is going to be a busy day at school.
Sandy isn't going to write with a _____
she is going to write with a _____ .
Lucy isn't going to color with _____ ;
she's going to color with _____ .
Tony isn't going to use a new _____ ;
he's going to use a new _____ .
Andy isn't going to borrow a _____ ;
he's going to borrow a _____ .
And, I am not going to work in the _____ ;
I am going to work in the _____ .
Yes, tomorrow is going to be a very busy day at school!

pen • pencil • eraser • sharpener • book
notebook • markers • color penciis
crayons • ruler

Future Tense Negative

We use **BE** + going to + verb to express a planned action in the future.

Negative sentences:
Subject +BE+ NOT+ going to+ verb.
She **is not** going to use a pencil.
They **are not** going to use and eraser.
I **am not** going to work in the notebook.

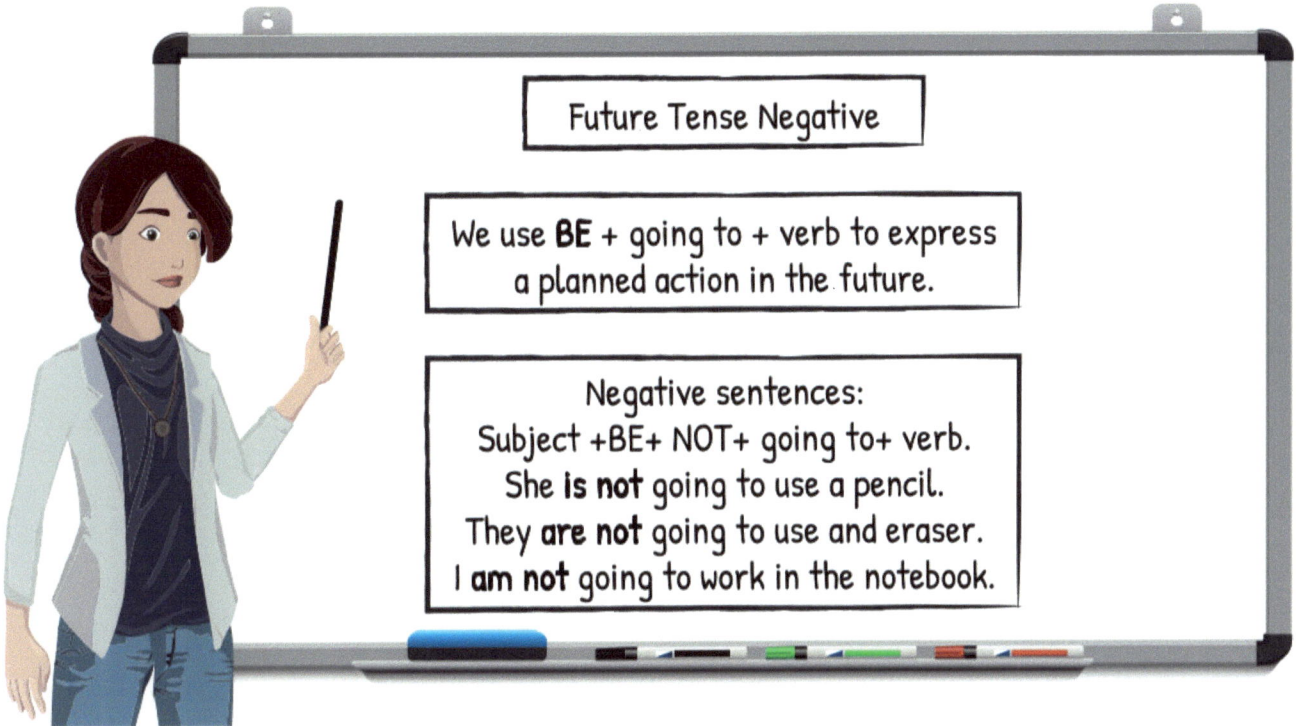

Answer the questions

1. Is Sandy going to write with a pen?
_____

2. Is Lucy going to color with crayons?
_____

3. Is Tony going to use a new eraser?
_____

4. Is Andy going to borrow a marker?
_____

5. Are you going to work in the notebook?
_____

Choose the correct negative form

1. She _____ going to color with crayons.
   a) isn't   b) aren't

2. They _____going to write with a pencil.
   a) isn't   b) aren't

3. He _____ to use a new eraser.
   a) am not b) isn't

4. We _____ going to borrow a marker.
   a) am not b) aren't

5. I _____ going to work in the book.
   a) aren't   b) am not

How well did you do in this unit?

Write the CAN DO statement and assess yourself:

I can...

Learn the names of the countries

Canada
England
Puerto Rico
China
South Africa
Australia

mountains

city

beach

Practice the dialogs

Where is Sandy going to go on her vacation?
-She is going to go to Puerto Rico.
Great! What is she going to do there?
-She's going to visit the beach.

Where are you going to go on your vacation?
-I am going to go to China.
Really? What are you going to do there?
-I'm going to visit the cities.

Where is Lucy going to go on her vacation?
-She is going to go to South Africa.
Awesome! What is she going to do there?
-She's going to visit the cities.

Where is Miss Patty going to go on her vacation?
-She's going to go to Australia.
Fantastic! What is she going to do there?
-She's going to visit the beach.

Where is Tony going to go on his vacation?
-He's going to go to Canada.
Great! What is he going to do there?
-He's to visit the mountains.

Where is _____ going to go
on his/her vacation?
-He's/She's going to go
to _____.
Fantastic! What is he/she
going to do there?
-He/ She's going to visit _____.

Now you!

Our next vacation

Miss Patty says that we are going to travel all around the world for our next vacation, well, with our imagination!
Andy is going to go to China; he's going to visit the cities.
Sandy is going to go to Puerto Rico; she's going to visit the beach.
Lucy is going to go to South Africa; she's going to visit the cities.
Tony is going to go to Canada; he's going to visit the mountains.
Miss Patty is going to go to Australia; she's going to visit the beach.
Yes, we are going to have awesome vacations, in our imagination!
Where are you going on your next vacation?

Where are they going ?

1. Who is going to go to China?
   ☐ Andy   ☐ Lucy   ☐ Tony

2. Who is going to go to Canada?
   ☐ Miss Patty ☐ Lucy   ☐ Tony

3. Who is going to go to Australia?
   ☐ Miss Patty ☐ Tony   ☐ Andy

4. Who is going to go to Puerto Rico?
   ☐ Sandy   ☐ Lucy   ☐ Miss Patty

5. Who is going to go to South Africa?
   ☐ Andy   ☐ Tony   ☐ Lucy

Match the sentence halves

1. Andy is going to visit   (_____)

2. Sandy is going to visit   (_____)

3. Lucy is going to visit   (_____)

4. Tony is going to visit   (_____)

5. Miss Patty is going to visit(_____)

a) the beach in Australia.
b) the beach in Puerto Rico.
c) the cities in China.
d) the cities in South Africa.
e) the mountains in Canada.

Complete the reading with the words from the box below

Our next vacation

Miss Patty says that we are going to travel all around the world for our next vacation, well, with our imagination!

Andy is going to go to _____;
he's going to visit the _____.
Sandy is going to go to _____;
she's going to visit the _____.
Lucy is going to go to _____;
she's going to visit the _____.
Tony is going to go to _____;
he's going to visit the _____.
Miss Patty is going to go to _____;
she's going to visit the _____.
Yes, we are going to have awesome vacations, in our imagination!
Where are you going on your next vacation?

Canada • Puerto Rico • China • South Africa
mountains • cities • beach

Future Tense Wh- questions

We use **BE** + going to + verb to express a planned action in the future.

WH- questions
WH+ BE+ subject + going to+ verb.
Where is he going to go?
What are they going to do?

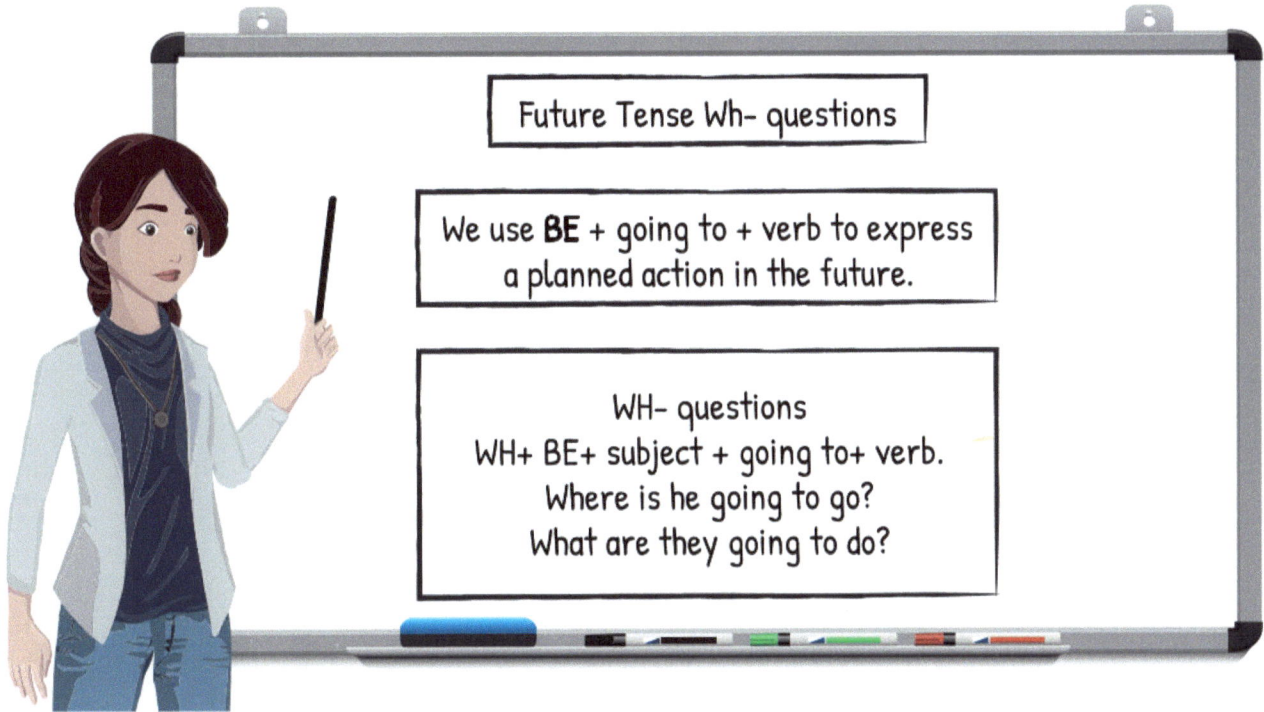

Unscramble the sentences

1. _____ _____ _____ _____ _____?
   Sandy / is / going to /where / go

2. _____ _____ _____ _____ _____?
   do / going to / Andy / is / what

3. _____ _____ _____ _____ _____?
   is / visit / who / China / going to

4. _____ _____ _____ _____ _____?
   Where / they / are / go / going to

Complete the questions. Answer them using the clues in parenthesis

1. _____ is going to visit China? (Lucy)

2. _____ is Andy going to go?(China)

3. _____ are they going to do there? (visit the cities)

4. _____ is going to visit Canada? (Sandy)

5. _____ is Lucy going to go? (South Africa)

6. _____ are you going to do there? (go to the beach)

How well did you do in this unit?

_____

Write the CAN DO statement and assess yourself:

I can...

_____

_____

_____

_____

_____

_____

_____

_____

Learn the school subjects

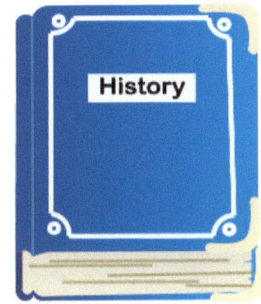

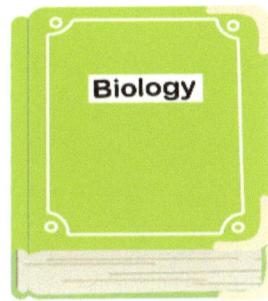

Learn the after school activities

go to the movies

listen to music

play video games

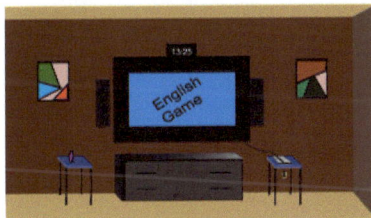

walk

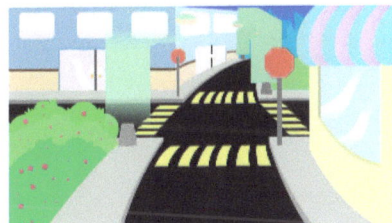

watch T.V.

Practice the dialogs

Can Tony go to the movies today?
-No, he can't. He has to study Math.

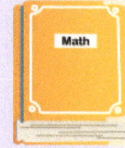

Can Lucy listen to music today?
-No, she can't. She has to study English.

Can Andy play video games today?
-No, he can't. He has to study Science.

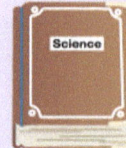

Can Sandy watch TV today?
-No, she can't. She has to study Biology.

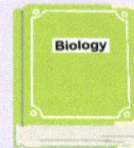

Can you go for a walk today?
-No, I can't. I have to prepare a history exam.

Now you!

Can _____ _____?
-No, she/he can't.
-She/he has to study _____.

Exams

My friends and I are very busy today.
We can't do our usual activities.
We have to study because we have exams this week!
Tony can't go to the movies; he has to study Math.
Sandy can't watch TV today; she has to study Biology.
Andy can't play video games; he has to study Science.
Lucy can't listen to music; she has to study English.
Even Miss Patty can't go for a walk;
she has to prepare a History exam!
We all have to study very hard today!
What do you have to study?

Choose true or false

1. Tony can't go to the movies. He has to study English.
   ❑ True   ❑ False
2. Sandy can't watch TV. She has to study Biology.
   ❑ True   ❑ False
3. Andy can't play video games. He has to study History.
   ❑ True   ❑ False
4. Lucy can't listen to music. She has to study Science.
   ❑ True   ❑ False
5. Miss Patty can't go for a walk. She has to study History.
   ❑ True   ❑ False

Choose the correct activity

1. Sandy has to study:
   ❑ Math ❑ Biology ❑ History
2. Andy has to study:
   ❑ Math ❑ Biology ❑ Science
3. Lucy has to study:
   ❑ English ❑ Math ❑ History
4. Tony has to study:
   ❑ English ❑ Math ❑ History
5. Miss Patty has to study:
   ❑ English ❑ Science ❑ History

Complete the reading with the words from the box below

Exams

My friends and I are very busy today.
We can't do our usual activities.
We have to study because we have exams this week!
Tony can't _____; he has to study _____.
Sandy can't _____ today; she has to study _____.
Andy can't _____; he has to study _____.
Lucy can't _____; she has to study _____.
Even Miss Patty can't _____;
she has to prepare a _____ exam!
We all have to study very hard today!
What do you have to study?

---

go to the movies • listen to music • play video games
watch TV • walk

Math • History • Biology • English • Science

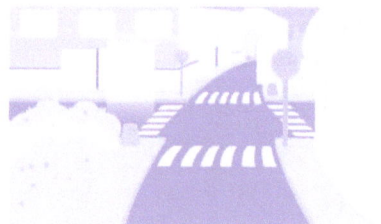

We use **have to** and **has to**, to express an obligation or a necessity.
We form sentences with **have to** and **has to** in the Present Simple tense
affirmative form: Subject+ have/has to+ verb
We use **have to** with: I, YOU, WE THEY
We use **has to** with: HE, SHE, IT

We use **CAN** in the Present Simple tense to express ability.
We use **CAN** with every subject: I/YOU/HE/SHE/IT/WE/THEY CAN.

To make interrogative sentences: **CAN** +subject+ verb (simple form)

To make negative sentences:
Subject+ **CAN + NOT** (can't)+ verb (simple form)

Answer the questions

1. Can Tony go to the movies?
No, ____ ____.
He ____ ____ study Math.

2. Can Andy play video games today?
No, ____ ____.
He ____ ____ study Science.

3. Can Lucy listen to music?
No, ____ ____.
She ____ ____ study English.

4. Can you go for a walk today?
No, ____ ____. I ____ ____ prepare a History exam.

How well did you do in this unit?

Write the CAN DO statement and assess yourself:

I can...

Learn the clothes and the weather

raincoat

boots

shorts

sweater

jacket

Practice the dialogs

Do I have to wear a raincoat?
-Yes, you do. It's rainy.

Do Andy and Tony have to wear sweaters?
-Yes, they do. It's cloudy.

Does Tony have to wear boots?
-Yes, he does. It's snowy.

Does Lucy have to wear shorts?
-Yes, she does. It's sunny.

Do you and Sandy have to wear jackets?
-Yes, we do. It's windy.

Now you!

Do/Does _____ have to wear _____?
-Yes, _____ _____ . It's _____ .

Different clothes for different weather

Our teacher, Miss Patty, says that we have to wear different clothes for different kinds of weather.
She says that, we have to wear a jacket when it's windy.
We have to wear a raincoat when it's rainy. We have to wear a sweater when it's cloudy. We have to wear boots when it's snowy. And we have to wear shorts when it's sunny. Well, it is sure a lot to remember, but we are happy because we have Miss Patty to tell us what clothes to wear in different kinds of weather.
What do you have to wear today?

Circle (✔) for true
Circle (✘) for false

Choose the correct clothes

1. It's rainy.
   I have to wear shorts.
   ✔ ✘

2. It's cloudy.
   They have to wear a sweater.
   ✔ ✘

3. It's snowy.
   He has to wear sweater.
   ✔ ✘

4. It's sunny.
   She has to wear a raincoat.
   ✔ ✘

5. It's windy.
   We have to wear jackets.
   ✔ ✘

1. It's rainy. I have to wear ____.
   • sweater   • raincoat   • jacket

2. It's cloudy. They have to wear ____.
   • sweater   • raincoat   • shorts

3. It's snowy. He has to wear ____.
   • shorts   • raincoat   • boots

4. It's sunny. She has to wear ____.
   • shorts   • raincoat   • boots

5. It's windy. We have to wear ____.
   • boots   • jackets   • shorts

Complete the reading with the words from the box below

Different clothes for different weather

Our teacher, Miss Patty, says that we have to wear different clothes for different kinds of weather.
She says that, we have to wear a _____ when it's _____. We have to wear a _____ when it's _____. We have to wear a _____ when it's _____. We have to wear _____ when it's _____.
And we have to wear _____ when it's _____. Well, it is sure a lot to remember, but we are happy because we have Miss Patty to tell us what clothes to wear in different kinds of weather.
What do you have to wear today?
It's _____ I have to wear _____!

shorts • sweater • boots • jackets • raincoat (x2)
sunny • cloudy • snowy • windy • rainy (x2)

We use **have** to and **has to**, to express an obligation or a necessity.
We form sentences with **have to** and **has to**
in the *Present Simple* tense *interrogative form:*
Do/does+ Subject+ have to+ verb

We use **do/ have to** with: I, you, we, they
Do you **have to** wear a raincoat?

We use **does /have to** with: he, she, it
Does she **have to** wear boots?

Complete the questions using the correct form of have to

1. _____ I _____ _____ wear a raincoat?

2. _____ Andy and Tony _____ _____ wear sweaters?

3. _____ Tony _____ _____ wear boots?

4. _____ Lucy _____ _____ wear shorts?

5. _____ you _____ _____ wear a sweater?

Complete clothes crosswords across

1   2   3

4   5   6

7

8 1

2   10

3

4   9

5

6

down

7   8

9   10

59

How well did you do in this unit?

_____

Write the CAN DO statement and assess yourself:

I can...

_____

_____

_____

_____

_____

_____

Learn the names of the clothes and the seasons of the year

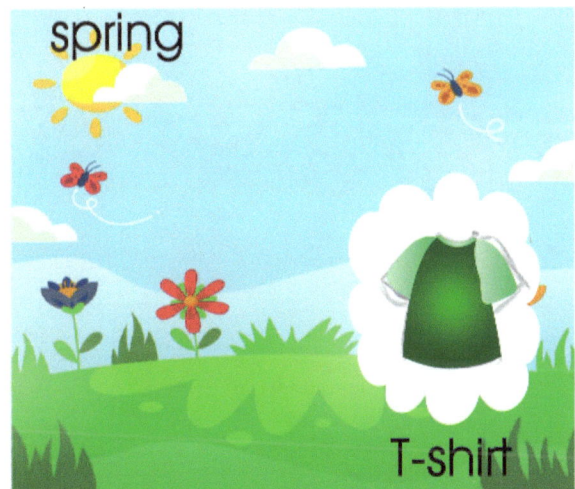

summer

swimsuit

fall

scarf

winter

gloves

spring

T-shirt

Practice the dialogs

I think I have to wear a scarf in the spring!
-Don't be silly!
You don't have to wear a scarf.
It's warm in the spring.

I think I have to wear gloves in the summer!
-Don't be silly!
You don't have to wear gloves.
It's hot in the summer.

I think I have to wear a swimsuit in the winter.
Don't be silly!
You don't have to wear a swimsuit.
It's cold in the winter.

I think I have to wear a T-shirt in the fall.
-Don't be silly!
You don't have to wear a T-shirt.
It's cool in the fall.

Now you!

I think I have to wear a_____ in the _____.
Don't be silly!
You don't have to wear a _____.
It's _____ in the _____.

Silly clothes for different seasons

Today we are playing "dress up"
but we are being silly with clothes
that we have to wear in the different seasons.
Sandy chooses to wear gloves in the summer!
Miss Patty says: "Of course you can wear them,
but you don't have to wear gloves
because in the summer it is hot."
Andy chooses to wear a scarf in the spring!
"You don't have to wear a scarf because
in the spring it is warm."
Tony chooses to wear a swimsuit in the winter!
"You don't have to wear a swimsuit because
it is cold in the winter."
Lucy chooses to wear a T-shirt in the fall!
You don't have to wear a T-shirt because it is cool in the fall."
You don't have to wear silly clothes, but if you want to…
have fun!

Match sentences 1-4 with a-d

1) It's hot in the _____.
2) It's cold in the _____.
3) It's cool in the _____.
4) It's warm in the _____.

a)  b)

c)  d)

Circle true or false

1. You don't have to wear gloves in the winter	true	false
2. You don't have to wear a swimsuit in the summer	true	false
3. You don't have to wear a scarf in the spring	true	false
4. You don't have wear a T-shirt in the fall	true	false

Complete the reading with the words from the box below

Silly clothes for different seasons

Today we are playing "dress up" but we are being silly with clothes
that we have to wear in the different seasons.
Sandy chooses to wear _____ in the _____! Miss Patty says:
"Of course you can wear that, but you don't have to."
Andy chooses to wear a _____ in the _____! "Of course you
can wear that, but you don't have to."
Tony chooses to wear a _____ in the _____! "Of course you
can wear that, but you don't have to."
Lucy chooses to wear a _____ in the _____! "Of course you
can wear that, but you don't have to."
You don't have to wear silly clothes, but if you want to…
have fun!

winter • spring • summer • fall
gloves • t-shirt • swimsuit • scarf

We use **have to** and **has to**, to express an obligation or a necessity.
We form sentences with **have to** and **has to** in
the *Present Simple* tense *negative* form:
Subject+ do/does+ not+ have to+ verb

We use **do not/ have to** with: I, you, we, they
You **don't have to** wear gloves in the summer.

We use **does not /have to** with: he, she, it
She **doesn't have to** wear a swimsuit in the winter.

Complete the words for clothes and seasons

1. f ___ ___ ___

2. g ___ ___ ___ ___ s

3. s ___ ___ ___ f

4. s ___ ___ ___ ___ g

5. s ___ ___ ___ ___ r

6. s ___ ___ m ___ ___ ___ t

7. T - ___ ___ ___ ___ t

8. w ___ ___ ___ ___ r

Unscramble the sentences

1. _____ _____ _____ _____
   _____ .
   a scarf / have to / you / don't / wear

2. _____ _____ _____ _____
   _____ .
   a swimsuit / she / have to / doesn't / wear

3. _____ _____ _____ _____
   _____ .
   a T-shirt / don't / have to / wear / they

4. _____ _____ _____ _____
   _____ .
   doesn't / wear / have to / gloves / he

How well did you do in this unit?

_____

Write the CAN DO statement and assess yourself:

I can...

_____

_____

_____

_____

_____

_____

Learn days of the week and months of the year

1	2	3	4	5	6	7
Sunday	Monday	Tuesday	Wednesday	Thursday	Friday	Saturday

1	2	3	4	5	6
January	February	March	April	May	June

7	8	9	10	11	12
July	August	September	October	November	December

THANK YOU

MAY I?

EXCUSE ME

You're welcome

I'M SORRY

PLEASE

Don't worry

May I borrow...?

Let me help you

Practice the dialogs

Excuse me, how do you spell
OCTOBER?
-With a capital
  "O-c-t-o-b-e-r."
Thank you.
-You're welcome.

Excuse me, may I borrow
your pencil?
-Sure!
Thanks.
-Don't worry.

I'm sorry, how do you spell
MONDAY?
-With a capital
  "M-o-n-d-a-y."
Thanks.
-Don't worry.

May I borrow your marker,
please?
-Of course!
Thank you.
-You're welcome.

Excuse me, how do you spell
DECEMBER?
-With a capital
  "D-e-c-e-m-b-e-r."
Thank you.
-Sure.

Excuse me; may I borrow
your book?
-Sure!
Thanks.
-You're welcome.

Now you!

Excuse me, how do you spell _____?
-With a capital "_ _ _ _ _ _ _ _ _ _ _ _"
Thanks.
-You're welcome.

Excuse me; may I borrow your _____?
-Sure!
Thanks.
-You're welcome.

THANK YOU

EXCUSE ME

Magic words

Miss Patty says that there are some beautiful words
that we have to use every day. She calls them "Magic Words";
she says that when we use them everything is better, like MAGIC!
For example, if you don't have a pencil, you don't just grab it.
You can say: May I borrow your pencil? And then your friend
is not going to be angry, he is going to let you use
his pencil! Isn't it like magic?

Let me help you

MAY I?

When you want to come into the classroom,
if you say: May I come in? Miss Patty is going to be very happy;
she is going to answer: "Sure!" You see, just like magic!
There are other Magic Words like: please, excuse me, I'm sorry,
don't worry; and Miss Patty's favorite: Let me help you!
She is always so nice!

I'M SORRY

PLEASE

Well, remember to always use Magic Words
and everything is going to be MAGICAL!

You're welcome   *Don't worry*   *May I borrow...?*

Choose the best magic word to complete the expressions

1. May I borrow your pencil?
   - ❑ You're welcome
   - ❑ May I come in?
   - ❑ Of course!

2. May I come in?
   - ❑ Sure!
   - ❑ You're welcome
   - ❑ Thank you!

3. Let me help you!
   - ❑ Thank you.
   - ❑ I'm sorry
   - ❑ May I come in?

4. _____ , may I borrow your pencil?
   - ❑ Thanks
   - ❑ You're welcome
   - ❑ Excuse me

Choose a word from the box below and fill in a blank. Then read aloud.

Magic words

In class every day we use special words,
they are called "Magic Words."
For example: _____, _____,
and _____.
We also use _____
Miss Patty says: _____
There are other Magic Words like:
_____, _____, _____ and _____.
My favorite word is: _____.
I am going to use Magic Words every day in school and at home.

What is your favorite Magic Word?

Excuse me • Thank you • You're welcome • Please
I'm sorry • May I come in? • Let me help you
May I borrow? • Don't worry • Sure

THANK YOU   EXCUSE ME   May I?

Let me help you   I'M SORRY   PLEASE

You're welcome   Don't worry

We use capital letters at the beginning of:
Days of the week
Sunday, Monday, Tuesday
Tomorrow is going to be Monday.

Months of the year:
January, February, March

Complete the days of the week

1. ___ unday

2. ___ onday

3. T_____

4. W_____

5. ___ hursday,

6. F_____

7. _____ .

Complete the months of the year

1. ___ anuary

2. ___ ebruary

3. M_____

4. ___ pril

5. _____

6. J_____

7. _____ uly

8. A_____

9. _____ eptember

10. Oct_____

11. N_____

12. _____

How well did you do in this unit?

_____

Write the CAN DO statement and assess yourself:

I can...

_____

_____

_____

_____

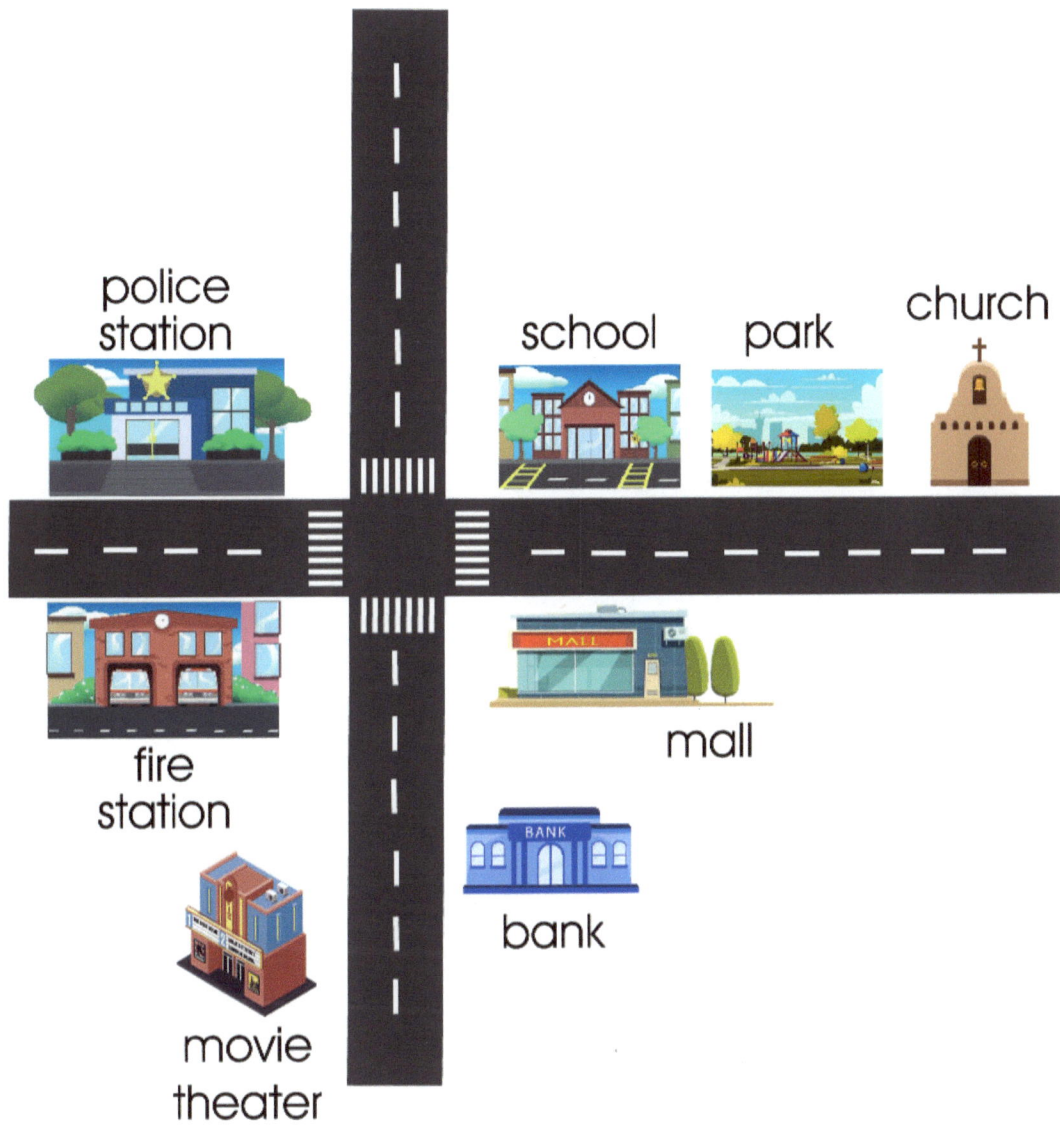

police
station

school

park

church

fire
station

mall

bank

movie
theater

→ next to

------▶ across from

→ ← between

Practice the dialogs

Excuse me, where is the mall?
-It's across from the park.
Thank you.
-Sure!

Excuse me, where is the school?
-It's next to the park.
Thanks.
-Sure.

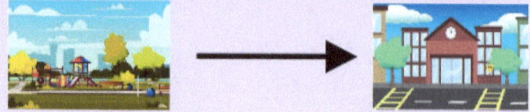

Excuse me, where is the fire station?
-It's across from the police station.
Thank you.
-Don't worry.

Excuse me, where is the bank?
-It's across from the movie theater.
Thank you.
-You're welcome.

Sorry, where is the park?
-It's between the church and the school.
Thanks a lot.
-You're welcome.

Now you!

Excuse me, where is the _____?
-It's _____.
Thank you.
-You're welcome

My town

I live in a beautiful town. My mom and dad take me everywhere.
And now, I can tell my friends where everything is.
For example; the mall, my favorite place in town,
is across from the park; I love to go to the mall
and then to the park on Saturdays.
The park is between the church and the school.
I can see the park from the window in my classroom.
The police station is just across from the fire station.
The bank is across from the movie theater.
I love my town. My town is beautiful!
Is your town beautiful? Do you know where everything is?

Choose **True** if the sentences are correct. **False** if the sentences are incorrect.

1. The mall is across from the fire station.
   ❑ True ❑ False
2. The park is across from the mall.
   ❑ True ❑ False
3. The church is between the school and the park.
   ❑ True ❑ False
4. The movie theater is next to the bank.
   ❑ True ❑ False

Match sentences 1-5 with images a-e

• The mall is across from the _____.
• The park is between the school and the _____.
• The park is next to the _____.
• The movie theater is across from the _____
• The fire station is across from the _____.

a b c d e

Choose a word from the box below and fill in a blank. Then read aloud.

My town

I live in a beautiful town. My mom and dad take me everywhere.
And now, I can tell my friends where everything is.
For example: the _____, my favorite place in town,
is across from the _____.
The _____ is between the _____ and the _____.
The _____ is just across from the _____.
The _____ is across from the _____.
I love my town. My town is beautiful!
Is your town beautiful? Do you know where everything is?

---

fire station • police station • church • school
mall • park • bank • movie theater

We use the imperative form to give directions.

We use the prepositions: **next to, across from and between** to express the relation of places to give directions.

On the corner **turn right**. The school is **across from** the mall.

Turn left on the corner. The mall is **next to** the park.

Turn right on the corner. The movie theater is **between** the school and the park.

Unscramble the sentences

1. _____ _____ _____ _____.
   next to / is / the school the park

2. _____ _____ _____ _____ _____.
   right / the / on / corner turn

3. _____ _____ _____ _____ _____.
   The park / between / is the church / and mall

4. _____ _____ _____ _____ _____.
   corner / the / on / left / turn

5. _____ _____ _____ _____.
   the mall / across from / is the bank

Time to Rhyme

Wee Willie Winkie
Runs through the town,
Upstairs and downstairs,
In his nightgown,
Tapping at the window,
Crying through the lock,
Are all the children in their beds?
It's past eight o'clock!

How well did you do in this unit?

Write the CAN DO statement and assess yourself:

I can...

Learn the names of the toys

toy car

truck

blocks

train

teddy bear

doll

bike

ball

jump rope

Practice the dialogs

Is Andy going to play with his train?
-No, he isn't.
-He's going to play with his blocks.

Are you going to play with your Teddy Bear?
-No, I'm not. I'm going to ride my bike.

Is Sandy going to play with her ball?
-No, she isn't.
-She's going to play with her Teddy Bear.

Are Lucy and Sandy going to play with their dolls?
-No, they aren't. They're going to play with their jump ropes.

Are you and Tony going to play with your toy cars?
-No, we aren't.
-We are going to play with our trucks.

Now you!

Is / Are _____ going to play with _____ _____ ?
-No, _____ _____. _____ going to play with _____ _____.

What are you going to play with?

Tomorrow is going to be Saturday,
and all my friends and I want to play all day long.
But, what are we going to play with?
Andy isn't going to play with his train; he's going to play
with his blocks. Lucy isn't going to play with her dolls;
she's going to play with her jump rope.
Tony isn't going to play with his toy cars;
he's going to play with his trucks.
Sandy isn't going to play with her ball;
she's going to play with her Teddy bear.
And I'm not going to play with my jump rope;
I'm going to play with my ball.
Yes, my friends and I are going to have fun tomorrow!

What are you going to play with?

What are you going to play with?

1. What is Andy going to play with?
   ❑ blocks ❑ train ❑ ball

2. What is Sandy going to play with?
   ❑ ball ❑ teddy bear ❑ jump rope

3. What is Lucy going to play with?
   ❑ dolls ❑ trucks ❑ jump rope

4. What is Tony going to play with?
   ❑ trucks ❑ bike ❑ toy cars

5. What are you going to play with?
   ❑ jump rope ❑ ball ❑ train

Circle (✔) if the sentence is correct (✘) if it's incorrect

1. Sandy isn't going to play with her Teddy bear.
   ✔ True   ✘ False

2. Tony is going to play with his trucks.
   ✔ True   ✘ False

3. I am not going to play with jump rope.
   ✔ True   ✘ False

4. Andy is going to play with his train.
   ✔ True   ✘ False

5. Lucy isn't going to play with her jump rope.
   ✔ True   ✘ False

Complete the reading with the words from the box below.
Then read aloud.

What are you going to play with?
Tomorrow is going to be Saturday,
and all my friends and I want to play all day long.
But, what are we going to play with?
Andy isn't going to play with his _____ ;
he's going to play with his _____ .
Lucy isn't going to play with her _____ ;
she's going to play with her _____ .
Tony isn't going to play with his _____ ;
he's going to play with _____ .
Sandy isn't going to play with her _____ ;
she's going to play with her _____ .
And you, what are YOU going to play with?
I'm not going to play with my _____ ;
I'm going to play with my _____ .

Yes, my friends and I are going to have fun tomorrow!

toys • bike • jump rope • toy car
doll • teddy bear • blocks • truck • train • ball

We use BE + going to + verb to express a planned action in the future.

We use the Possessive Adjectives to indicate ownership.
*Note that the possessive adjective does not change if you own one or several things.

I=my
you=your
he=his
she=her
it=its
we=our
they=their

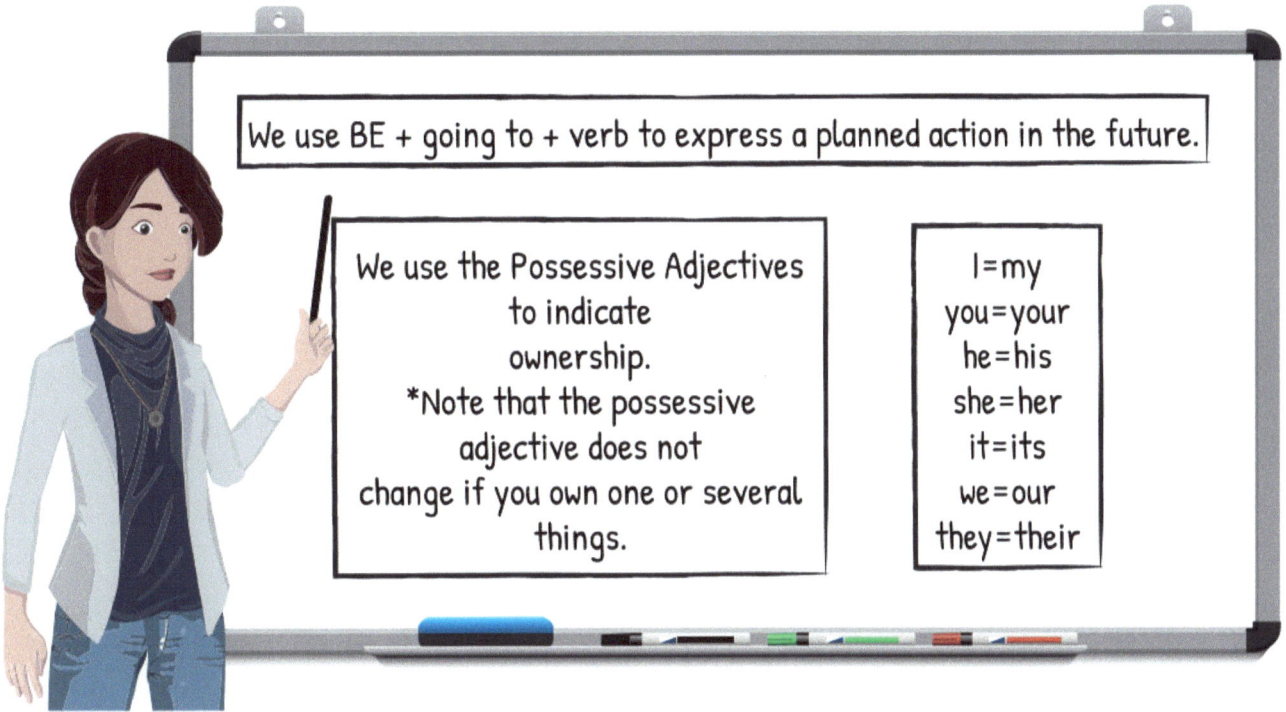

Complete the sentences with the correct possessive adjective

1. Andy is going to play with _____ train.

2. Sandy isn't going to play with _____ dolls.

3. Tony and Andy aren't going to play with _____ toy cars.

4. Lucy and I are going to play with _____ jump ropes.

5. I'm not going to play with _____ ball.

6. You are going to play with _____ Teddy bear.

my • your • his • her • our • their

Give a short answer

1. Is Andy going to play with the train?
   -No, _____ _____.

2. Is Sandy going to play with the dolls?
   -Yes, _____ _____.

3. Are Tony and Andy going to play with the toy cars?
   -No, _____ _____.

4. Are you and Lucy going to play with the jump ropes?
   -Yes, _____ _____.

5. Are you going to play with the ball?
   -No, _____ _____.

How well did you do in this unit?

_____

Write the CAN DO statement and assess yourself:

I can...
_____
_____
_____
_____
_____
_____

Learn the names of the food

milk

soup

hot dogs

spaghetti

hamburger

pizza

fries

bread

cookies

eggs

Complete the food words

1. m___ ___ k
2. b___ ___ ___ d
3. c___ ___ k ___ ___ ___
4. e___ ___ s
5. s ___ ___ p

6. h ___ ___ b ___ ___ g ___ ___
7. f___ ___ ___ s
8. h ___ ___ d___ ___ s
9. p ___ ___ ___ a
10. s ___ ___ ___ ___ h ___ ___ ___ i.

Practice the dialogs

What are you going to eat?
-I'm going to eat cookies.
Do you want milk too?
-Yes, thanks.
✓ ✓

What are you going to eat?
-I'm going to eat spaghetti.
Do you want pizza too?
-Yes, please.
✓ ✓

What are you going to eat?
-I'm going to eat eggs.
Do you want bread too?
-Sure, thanks.
✓ ✓

What are you going to eat?
-I'm going to eat hot dogs.
Do you want soup too?
-No, thanks.
✓ ✗

What are you going to eat?
-I'm going to eat hamburger.
Do you want fries too?
-No, thanks.
✓ ✗

Now you!

What are you going to eat?
-I'm going to eat _____.
Do you want _____ too?
-No, thanks. / Yes, please.

Delicious Food

My friends and I are always hungry
when we get home from school.
Right now we are thinking
what we are going to eat this afternoon.
Sandy is going to eat cookies and milk.
Andy is going to eat spaghetti and pizza.
Lucy is going to eat eggs and bread.
Harry is going to eat a hamburger.
Tony is going to eat hot dogs.
We love to get home and eat delicious food.
Thank you mom! Thank you dad!
What are you going to eat?

Who is going to eat?
Sandy/Andy/Lucy/Tony/Harry

Circle True if the sentence is correct.
False if the sentence is incorrect.

1. Who is going to eat a
   hamburger?
   _____

2. Who is going to eat spaghetti
   and pizza?
   _____

3. Who is going to eat cookies
   and milk?
   _____

4. Who is going to eat eggs and
   bread?
   _____

5. Who is going to eat hot dogs?
   _____

1. Andy is going to eat spaghetti
   and pizza.
   True   False

2. Sandy is going to eat eggs and
   bread.
   True   False

3. Lucy is going to eat cookies and
   milk.
   True   False

4. Harry is going to eat a hamburger.
   True   False

5. Tony is going to eat soup.
   True   False

Complete the reading with the words from the box below

Delicious Food

My friends and I are always hungry
when we get home from school.
Right now we are thinking what we are going to eat
this afternoon. Sandy is going to eat _____ and _____.
Andy is going to eat _____ and _____.
Lucy is going to eat _____ and _____.
Harry is going to eat a ____ and _____.
Tony is going to eat ____ and _____.
We love to get home and eat delicious food.
Thank you mom! Thank you dad!
What are you going to eat?
I am going to eat_____ and _____.,

eggs • bread • cookies • milk • spaghetti • pizza
hot dogs • hamburger • soup • fries

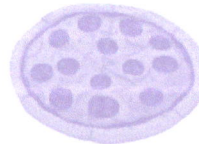

FUTURE TENSE

We use BE + going to + verb to express a planned action in the future.

We use **WH** – questions to ask for specific information.
Who = a person
What = a thing or action
When = a time
Where = a place

We form WH question in the future tense:
Wh+ be+ going to+ subject+ verb +complement?
What is Andy going to eat?

Complete the sentences with the WH question word Who/ What/ Where/ When

1. _____ is Andy going to eat? (pizza)

2. _____ is going to eat pizza? (Sandy)

3. _____ are you going to eat cookies? (tomorrow)

4. _____ are they going to eat hamburgers? (in the kitchen)

Unscramble the sentences

1. _____ _____ _____ _____ _____ ?
What/ Andy/ going to/ is/ eat

2. _____ _____ _____ _____ _____ ?
going to/ is / who/ pizza/eat

3. _____ _____ _____ _____ _____
_____ ?
cookies/eat/ going to/ are when/you

4. _____ _____ _____ _____
_____ ?
they/going to/ hamburgers eat/when/are

How well did you do in this unit?

Write the CAN DO statement and assess yourself:

I can...

Learn the names of games and sports

soccer

football

basketball

baseball

volley ball

swimming

chess

checkers

jumping rope

tag

Practice the dialogs

Are you going to play chess?
-No, I'm not.
What are you going to play?
-I think I'm going to play checkers.
Great! Can I play too?

Are you and Michelle going to jump rope?
-No, we aren't.
What are you going to play?
-Perhaps we're going to play tag.
Great! Can I play too?

Are Tony and Harry going to play soccer?
-No, they aren't.
What are they going to play?
-I guess they're going to play football.
Great! Can I play too?

Is Sandy going to play volleyball?
-No, she isn't.
What is she going to play?
-I think she's going to go swimming.
Great! Can I go too?

Now you!

Is Sandy going to play _____?
-No, she isn't.
What is she going to play?
-I think she's going to go _____.
Great! Can I _____ too?

Stay healthy!

Miss Patty says that when we play sports we keep our bodies healthy.
Also, when we practice games our minds stay healthy too.
So this week we are going to play sports and games.
I am going to play checkers; I'm not going to play chess.
Lucy and Michelle are going to play tag;
they aren't going to jump rope.
Tony and Harry are going to play football;
they aren't going to play soccer.
And Sandy isn't going to play volleyball;
she's going to go swimming.
As you can see we are going to have a healthy week,
playing games and sports. What are you going to play?
Stay healthy!

What are they going to play?

1. What are you going to play?
❑ chess ❑ tag ❑ checkers

2. What are Lucy and Michelle going to play?
❑ tag ❑ jump rope ❑ swimming

3. What are Tony and Harry going to play?
❑ soccer ❑ volleyball ❑ football

4. What is Sandy going to play?
❑ volleyball ❑ swimming
❑ soccer

Match 1-4 with a-d

1) Andy isn't going to play _____.

2) Lucy and Michelle aren't going to _____.

3) Tony and Harry aren't going to play _____.

4) Sandy isn't going to play _____.

a   b   c   d

Complete the reading with the words from the box below.
Then read aloud.

Stay healthy!

Miss Patty says that when we play sports we keep our bodies healthy.
Also, when we practice games our minds stay healthy too.
So this week we are going to play sports and games.
I am going to play _____; I'm not going to play _____.
Lucy and Michelle are going to play _____;
they aren't going to play _____.
Tony and Harry are going to play _____;
they aren't going to play _____.
And Sandy isn't going to play _____;
she's going to play _____.
As you can see we are going to have a healthy week,
playing games and sports.
What are you going to play? I am going to play_____.
Stay healthy!

soccer • football • basketball • baseball • volley ball
swimming • chess • checkers • jump rope • tag

FUTURE TENSE

We use BE + going to + verb to express a planned action in the future.
We use **WH** – questions to ask for specific information.
Who = a person
What = a thing or action

We form **WH** question in the future tense:
Wh+ be+ subject+ going to+ verb +complement?
What is Andy going to play?
Who is going to go swimming?

Unscramble the sentences

1. ____ ____ ____ ____ ____ ?
   is/ going to/ play/soccer/who

2. ____ ____ ____ ____ ____ ?
   Sandy/ going to/is/what/play

3. ____ ____ ____ ____ ____ ?
   Tony and Harry/ going to play/are/what

4. ____ ____ ____ ____ ____ ?
   you/going to/ are/what /play

Complete the answers

1. What are you going to play?
   -I ____ going to play ____.

2. What are you and Michelle going to play?
   -We ____ going to play ____.

3. What are Tony and Harry going to play?
   -They ____ going to play ____.

4. What is Sandy going to play?
   -She ____ going to play ____.

How well did you do in this unit?

Write the CAN DO statement and assess yourself:

I can...

REFERENCES

• Communicative Language Learning. Retrieved August 23, 2019 from:
  http://www.educationbridge-id.com/news-a-article/72-communicative-language-teaching-clt.html

• Brown, H. Douglas (1994). Principles of Language Learning and Teaching. Prentice Hall.

• Beale, Jason (2008). Is communicative language teaching a thing of the past?. TESOL article.

• Harmer, Jeremy (2007). How to teach English. Pearson Longman.

• Richards, Jack C (2002). Methodology in Language Teaching. Cambridge University Press.

• Willis, Jane (1996). A Framework for Task-Based Learning. Longman.

• Hermitt, A. (2015). Spiral Learning, a superior approach? In Families.com. Retrieved January
  9th, 2015, from http://www.families.com/blog/spiral-learning-a-superior approach.

• Fleming, N. Baume, D. (2006) Learning Styles.

• Again: VARKing up the right tree! , Educational Developments, SEDA Ltd, Issue 7.4 Nov. 2006.

• Harmer, Jeremy. How to Teach English. Harlow: Longman, 1998. Krashen, Stephen D., and
  Terrell, Tracy D. The Natural Approach. Oxford: Pergamon, 1983.

• Sökmen, Anita J. "Current Trends in Teaching Second Language Vocabulary". In Vocabulary:
  *Description, Ac*quisition and Pedagogy, edited by N. Schmitt and M. McCarthy, 237-257
  England: Cambridge University Press, 1997.

• Snow, Marguerite Ann. "T*eaching English as a Second or Foreign Language". In* Content-Based
  and Immersion Models for Second and Foreign Language Teaching" Edited by M. Celce-Murcia.
  Heinle & Heinle Thomson Learning, 2001.

• Roth, Genevieve. Te*aching Very Young Children. Ric*hmond Handbooks for English Teachers.
  London: Richmond Publishing. 1998.

ABOUT THE AUTHOR

Patricia Avila has been an English teacher for more than 45 years in her native Tijuana, B. C. She has a Bachelor's in Education from the National Pedagogical University (UPN).

Her experience as a teacher ranges from Kindergarten to Masters. She has functioned as coordinator of Bachelor's in ESL Teaching, as well as for various other universities; she has also worked as an Academic Consultant for different Publishing Houses for more than 15 years. Her wide experience and love for young learners has given her the opportunity to share with you **MY ENGLISH ZONE THE BOOK**, a series that will enhance the learning of English in a dynamic and fun way.

www.ingramcontent.com/pod-product-compliance
Lightning Source LLC
Chambersburg PA
CBHW041053110426

42740CB00044B/53